W9-CRX-246

ANIMAL SAFARI

Sloths

by Megan Borgert-Spaniol

BELLWETHER MEDIA • MINNEAPOLIS, MN

Note to Librarians, Teachers, and Parents:

Blastoff! Readers are carefully developed by literacy experts and combine standards-based content with developmentally appropriate text.

Level 1 provides the most support through repetition of high-frequency words, light text, predictable sentence patterns, and strong visual support.

Level 2 offers early readers a bit more challenge through varied simple sentences, increased text load, and less repetition of high-frequency words.

Level 3 advances early-fluent readers toward fluency through increased text and concept load, less reliance on visuals, longer sentences, and more literary language.

Level 4 builds reading stamina by providing more text per page, increased use of punctuation, greater variation in sentence patterns, and increasingly challenging vocabulary.

Level 5 encourages children to move from "learning to read" to "reading to learn" by providing even more text, varied writing styles, and less familiar topics.

Whichever book is right for your reader, Blastoff! Readers are the perfect books to build confidence and encourage a love of reading that will last a lifetime!

This edition first published in 2016 by Bellwether Media, Inc.

No part of this publication may be reproduced in whole or in part without written permission of the publisher. For information regarding permission, write to Bellwether Media, Inc., Attention: Permissions Department, 5357 Penn Avenue South, Minneapolis, MN 55419.

Library of Congress Cataloging-in-Publication Data

Borgert-Spaniol, Megan, 1989- author.
  Sloths / by Megan Borgert-Spaniol.
     pages cm. – (Blastoff! Readers. Animal Safari)
  Summary: "Developed by literacy experts for students in kindergarten through grade three, this book introduces sloths to young readers through leveled text and related photos"– Provided by publisher.
  Audience: Ages 5-8
  Audience: K to grade 3
  Includes bibliographical references and index.
  ISBN 978-1-62617-214-2 (hardcover: alk. paper)
  1. Sloths–Juvenile literature. I. Title. II. Series: Blastoff! readers. 1, Animal safari.
  QL737.E2B67 2016
  599.3'13–dc23
                                                    2015003715

Printed in the United States of America, North Mankato, MN.

Contents

What Are Sloths?

Sloths are the slowest **mammals** in the world.

They live in
rain forests.
They spend
most of their
time in trees.

Tree Life

Sloths hang upside down. They **grip** branches with their long, curved **claws**.

claws

They curl up in trees to sleep. Their fur has **algae** on it to hide them from **predators**.

Sloths find food in trees. They eat leaves, twigs, and fruits.

Land and Water

Sloths do not move well on the ground. They pull themselves forward with their front claws.

They are good swimmers. They **paddle** with their long arms.

Baby Sloths

A female sloth
gives birth in a tree.
Her baby **clings**
to her chest.

Soon the baby can climb without mom. Hang in there, sloth!

Glossary

algae—green, plant-like material

claws—sharp, curved nails at the end of an animal's fingers and toes

clings—holds on tightly

grip—to grab tightly

mammals—warm-blooded animals that have backbones and feed their young milk

paddle—to move forward in water

predators—animals that hunt other animals for food

rain forests—warm, wet forests that get a lot of rain

To Learn More

AT THE LIBRARY

Carle, Eric. *"Slowly, Slowly, Slowly," Said the Sloth*. New York, N.Y.: Philomel Books, 2002.

Lunis, Natalie. *Three-toed Sloths: Green Mammals*. New York, N.Y.: Bearport, 2010.

Schuetz, Kari. *Baby Sloths*. Minneapolis, Minn.: Bellwether Media, 2014.

ON THE WEB

Learning more about sloths is as easy as 1, 2, 3.

1. Go to www.factsurfer.com.

2. Enter "sloths" into the search box.

3. Click the "Surf" button and you will see a list of related web sites.

With factsurfer.com, finding more information is just a click away.

Index

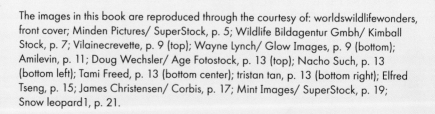

The images in this book are reproduced through the courtesy of: worldswildlifewonders, front cover; Minden Pictures/ SuperStock, p. 5; Wildlife Bildagentur Gmbh/ Kimball Stock, p. 7; Vilainecrevette, p. 9 (top); Wayne Lynch/ Glow Images, p. 9 (bottom); Amilevin, p. 11; Doug Wechsler/ Age Fotostock, p. 13 (top); Nacho Such, p. 13 (bottom left); Tami Freed, p. 13 (bottom center); tristan tan, p. 13 (bottom right); Elfred Tseng, p. 15; James Christensen/ Corbis, p. 17; Mint Images/ SuperStock, p. 19; Snow leopard1, p. 21.